CHOOSE HOPE,
TAKE ACTION

CHOOSE HOPE, TAKE ACTION

A Journal to Inspire and Empower

LORI ROBERTS

CHRONICLE BOOKS

SAN FRANCISCO

ISBN 978-1-4521-8020-5

Manufactured in China.

MIX
Paper from
responsible sources
FSC
www.fsc.org
FSC™ C136333

Design by Lizzie Vaughan and Katherine Yao.

10 9 8 7 6 5 4 3 2

Chronicle books and gifts are available at special quantity discounts to corporations, professional associations, literacy programs, and other organizations. For details and discount information, please contact our corporate/premiums department at corporatesales@chroniclebooks.com or at 1-800-759-0190.

Chronicle Books LLC
680 Second Street
San Francisco, California 94107
www.chroniclebooks.com

Around the globe, people are awakening to a changing reality and a greater sense of urgency to help make the world a better place. We want to feel hopeful in a world that seems increasingly unstable and downright scary at times. We watch the news, throw up our hands, and say, "Somebody needs to *do* something about this!" And we're ready for that somebody to be us.

But the continual bombardment of crisis after crisis—environmental disaster, mass shooting, political firestorm—can leave us feeling overwhelmed and numb. So we often do nothing.

A feeling of hopefulness and optimism for a better world can be cultivated by building a plan of action that will guide us toward a purpose. Because our personal happiness, and our ability to stay optimistic rather than give in to a feeling of helplessness, is linked to our actions, our desire to step up and make a difference.

So let's heed the call to do something that really matters in our lives, something that has an impact outside of ourselves, and challenge one another to find new ways to work for the greater good. This journal opens some space for exploration: What can I do when I feel powerless? What are my best qualities? What do I value? What brings me joy? Is there a place—or places—where my talents and desire to help the world can intersect? How can I make a difference in my own backyard and in the world beyond?

Whether it's feeding people, helping animals, calling your representative, or launching a nonprofit, there are a myriad of ways, big and small, in which we can help the world. Let's explore them together.

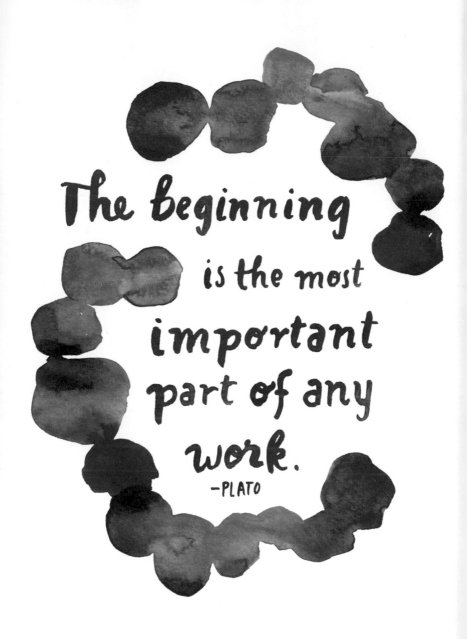

The beginning is the most important part of any work.
—PLATO

THE MAGIC OF BEGINNINGS

If you've picked up this journal, you want something to change.
In you? In your community? In your country? In the world?
Maybe you've felt a subtle shift in your outlook recently, a calling
to do something a little more meaningful in your life. Or maybe
an upcoming election is catapulting you forward into action. Are
you feeling an itch to make a difference and ready to begin? Why
is the time right for you to start this exploration? Why is this
important to you now?

_____

_____

_____

_____

_____

_____

_____

_____

_____

_____

_____

_____

_____

_____

_____

DO NOT WEEP; DO NOT WAX INDIGNANT. UNDERSTAND.

-BARUCH SPINOZA

DO NOT WEEP

At this point, you might have read one too many news headlines, and you're ready to either become a hermit or do something—anything—to feel better about the state of the world. We may not know yet what we want to *do*, but we know how we *feel*. So focus on the feeling for now, and leave the doing for later. Are you feeling discouraged about politics? Fearful about climate change? Hopeful about a new community center in your neighborhood? Joyful about upcoming plans for the weekend? Write about your feelings, good and bad, big and small, here:

_____

_____

_____

_____

_____

_____

_____

_____

_____

_____

_____

_____

I'M READY

Studies find that showing generosity and helping others actually makes us happier, healthier, and less stressed-out. So whether it's baking, writing, organizing, or wielding a hammer, consider the gifts that you have to share with the world.

MY STRENGTHS:

_____
_____
_____
_____
_____
_____
_____
_____
_____
_____
_____
_____

MY SKILLS:

_____
_____
_____
_____
_____
_____
_____
_____
_____
_____
_____
_____

MY EXPERIENCE:

_____
_____
_____
_____
_____
_____
_____
_____
_____
_____
_____
_____

I'm ready to share my gifts with the world.

WE HAVE
OUR
TO BEGIN
OVER

IT IN POWER THE WORLD AGAIN.

-THOMAS PAINE

AT FIRST PEOPLE REFUSE
TO BELIEVE THAT A STRANGE
NEW THING CAN BE DONE,
THEN THEY BEGIN TO HOPE IT
CAN BE DONE, THEN THEY SEE IT
CAN BE DONE — THEN IT IS
DONE AND ALL THE WORLD
WONDERS WHY IT WAS
NOT DONE CENTURIES AGO.

—FRANCES HODGSON BURNETT

STRANGE NEW THINGS

It takes courage to make changes in your life, especially if they're outside the norm. Like eating less meat, opting for public transit over owning a car, using less plastic . . . Are there changes that you'd like to make in your life that feel a bit uncomfortable? Why do you think that is?

_____

_____

_____

_____

_____

_____

_____

_____

_____

_____

_____

_____

_____

_____

_____

_____

START SMALL

When we feel overwhelmed by the woes of the world, it's not always clear what we can do to make a difference. So let's start small. Treating people with kindness is something we have within our power to do today and every day. List five random or not-so-random acts of kindness you could do this week:

1. _____

_____

2. _____

_____

3. _____

_____

4. _____

_____

5. _____

_____

_____

Let
us be kind
to one another,
for most of us
are fighting a
hard battle.

–IAN MACLAREN

🌲 COMMUNITY 🌲

FELLOWSHIP, COMMONALITY, KINSHIP

What does *building community* mean to you,
and is it important in your life? Why? Why is building
community important to the world?

_____

_____

_____

_____

_____

_____

_____

_____

_____

_____

_____

_____

_____

_____

_____

_____

_____

_____

THE
PURPOSE
of Life
is NOt to
be HAPPY —
but to MATTER,
to be
ProdUctiVE,
to Be
UseFUL, to
HAVe it MAKe
SOMe dIFFeRence
ThaT you liVed
At ALL.
~ LEO ROSTEN

THE PURPOSE OF LIFE

When you consider people you know who are living a life of
purpose, what is it about their way of living that inspires you?
What do you think it means to live well?

_____

_____

_____

_____

_____

_____

_____

_____

_____

_____

_____

_____

_____

_____

_____

_____

_____

_____

Let us not
look back in
ANGER,
nor forward in
FEAR,
but around in
AWARENESS.

—JAMES THURBER

PAY ATTENTION

Go about your day, but be aware. Really pay attention and try to discern what matters most to you—concerns about your family, a news article about veterans, or maybe something you notice while walking through your community. Don't worry about going into too much detail at this point; just brainstorm.

I'M CONCERNED ABOUT:

1. _____

2. _____

3. _____

4. _____

5. _____

6. _____

7. _____

8. _____

9. _____

10. _____

MY THANKSGIVING IS PERPETUAL

By regularly recognizing what we are grateful for,
big and small, we can cultivate feelings of hope
and optimism, and help prevent burnout. List
what you are thankful for today.

IN MY LIFE:

IN MY TOWN:

IN THE WORLD:

I am grateful for
what I am and have.
My thanksgiving is
perpetual. —HENRY
DAVID
THOREAU

Let the beauty of
what you love
be what you do.
-RUMI

FINDING MEANING

Our innermost desires are like compass points for finding meaning in our lives. How do you love to spend your free time? Are there certain activities or ways of expressing yourself that you're drawn to?

_____

_____

_____

_____

_____

_____

_____

_____

_____

_____

_____

_____

_____

_____

_____

_____

_____

BUT WE **are**

STRONG, each in our PURPOSE,

and we are all more **STRONG**

together.

—BRAM STOKER

THE BUDDY SYSTEM

Do you have a friend (or two) who might want to embark on this
exploration with you? What causes are you both interested in?
How might you challenge each other?

_____

_____

_____

_____

_____

_____

_____

_____

_____

_____

_____

_____

_____

_____

_____

_____

_____

WHAT YOU CAN DO,
OR DREAM YOU
CAN, BEGIN IT.
BOLDNESS HAS GENIUS,
POWER, AND MAGIC IN IT.

—JOHANN WOLFGANG VON GOETHE

THE WORLD'S BIG

What is something you've always wanted to do?
What's keeping you from doing it?

_____

_____

_____

_____

_____

_____

_____

_____

_____

_____

_____

_____

_____

_____

_____

_____

_____

_____

_____

IDEAS FOR WAYS TO NARROW YOUR FOCUS.

HOW DO I WANT TO HELP?

PEOPLE'S BASIC NEEDS (FOOD, CLOTHING, SHELTER):

- **VOLUNTEER AT A FOOD BANK.**

- **DONATE CLOTHING OR TOILETRIES TO A LOCAL HOMELESS SHELTER.**

All
happiness
depends
on
courage
and
work.
-Honoré de Balzac

COURAGE

What does *courage* mean to you, and is it
important in your life? Why? Why is courage
important to the world?

_____

_____

_____

_____

_____

_____

_____

_____

_____

_____

_____

_____

_____

_____

_____

_____

_____

EASING THEIR WAY

Explore five ways you could make life less
difficult for the people around you:

1. _____

_____

_____

2. _____

_____

_____

3. _____

_____

_____

4. _____

_____

_____

5. _____

_____

_____

what do we
live for,
if it is not
to make
life less
difficult for
each other?

-GEORGE ELIOT

BE SURE YOU
PUT YOUR
FEET IN THE
RIGHT PLACE,
THEN
STAND FIRM.

-ABRAHAM LINCOLN

STAND FIRM

Is there an issue you believe in so strongly that you're
prepared to take a stand for it? What are the risks of taking
a stand and committing to action? Are you the only one in
your family who believes in a certain cause? Do you feel that
you need more skills or information before you can take on
the issue of your choice? How are you prepared to move
forward despite these risks?

_____

_____

_____

_____

_____

_____

_____

_____

_____

_____

_____

_____

_____

FOUNTAINS OF LIFE

Studies show that spending time in nature has multiple health benefits, including lowering stress. Even if you live in the middle of an urban metropolis, you probably have at least *some* access to the natural world. Name five places in nature you could use as stress-busting sanctuaries on a regular basis:

1. _____

_____

2. _____

_____

3. _____

_____

4. _____

_____

5. _____

_____

_____

Thousands of tired, nerve-shaken, over-civilized people are beginning to find out that going to the mountains is going home.

—JOHN MUIR

COMMON GROUND

Chances are, if we talk to our parents or older friends about the greatest challenges of their time, they'll have plenty to share. How do they feel about the state of the world today? What is their perspective? Do you agree or disagree? If you disagree, are there any areas where you can find common ground?

_____

_____

_____

_____

_____

_____

_____

_____

_____

_____

_____

_____

_____

_____

_____

_____

THINK

OUTSIDE

THE

BOX

NEW PERSPECTIVES

Expanding our viewpoint can bring perspective, and show us how we connect to others around us and around the globe. Looking at the world outside your own city or country and taking the time to consider viewpoints other than your own is an exercise in empathy. How might this play out in your own life?

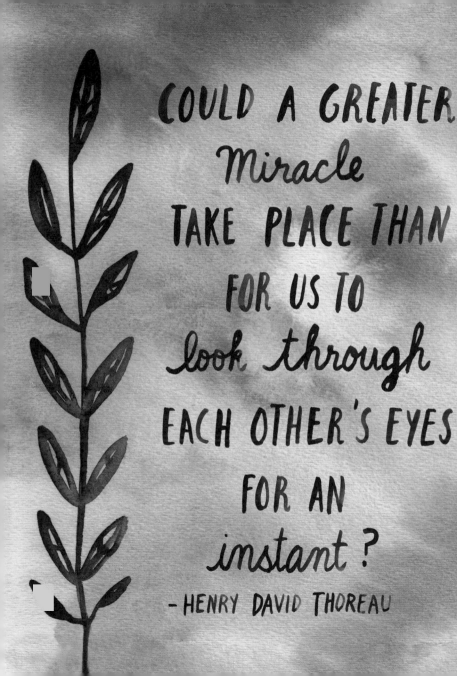

 EMPATHY

UNDERSTANDING, APPRECIATION, COMPASSION

What does *empathy* mean to you, and is it important in your life? Why? Why is empathy important to the world?

_____

_____

_____

_____

_____

_____

_____

_____

_____

_____

_____

_____

_____

_____

_____

_____

_____

_____

_____

_____

_____

WHEN YOU DO A THING,
DO IT WITH ALL YOUR
MIGHT. PUT YOUR
WHOLE SOUL INTO IT.

-RALPH WALDO
EMERSON

PUT YOUR WHOLE SOUL INTO IT

As the story goes, Sir Isaac Newton would get so engrossed in his work that he would forget to eat! What are some things you are passionate about? Sports? Politics? Travel? Cooking? Is there anything you are so passionate about that you might forget to eat?

_____

_____

_____

_____

_____

_____

_____

_____

_____

_____

_____

_____

_____

_____

_____

_____

_____

NOW ENVISION WAYS YOU COULD USE YOUR PASSIONS AS A FORCE FOR GOOD:

_____

_____

_____

_____

_____

_____

_____

_____

_____

_____

_____

_____

_____

_____

_____

_____

_____

_____

_____

_____

_____

There are dark shadows on the

stronger in the

DARK SHADOWS

In your view, where are the darkest shadows in the world?
What points of light or hope—people, organizations,
movements—do you see to contrast the darkness?
How do they inspire you? Why?

_____
_____
_____
_____
_____
_____
_____
_____
_____
_____
_____
_____
_____
_____

*earth, but its lights are
contrast.*
—CHARLES DICKENS

MY THANKSGIVING IS PERPETUAL

By regularly recognizing what we are grateful for,
big and small, we can cultivate feelings of hope
and optimism and help prevent burnout. List
what you are thankful for today.

IN MY LIFE:　　　**IN MY TOWN:**　　　**IN THE WORLD:**

It's not the length of life, but the depth of life.

-RALPH WALDO EMERSON

LETTER TO MY FUTURE SELF

Write a letter to your future self, and describe the life you hope
to live. What impact do you wish to make? What do you want
your legacy to be? Whom do you hope to inspire?

_____

_____

_____

_____

_____

_____

_____

_____

_____

_____

_____

_____

_____

_____

_____

_____

_____

_____

_____

If you want
to go QUICKLY,
go alone.
If you want
to go far . go
TOGETHER.

- PROVERB

WE'RE IN THIS TOGETHER

Consider some group activities you might be interested in or that you participate in already. Are there ways to bridge these interests with social engagement? Brainstorm some group activities that might have a positive impact:

BOOK CLUB
Choose books written by members of marginalized groups or that focus on nonfiction topics related to social justice.

SEWING CIRCLE
Donate quilts to hospitals, senior centers, or charitable organizations.

POTLUCK/BACKYARD BBQ
Encourage your guests to learn about and discuss issues that affect your town or area. Invite a community leader or local politician to address your group.

WALKATHON OR FUN RUN
Pick an important cause and encourage friends to participate.

IDEAS FOR WAYS TO NARROW YOUR FOCUS.

HOW DO I WANT TO HELP?

ANIMALS:

- DONATE TO AN ANIMAL WELFARE ORGANIZATION OR ANIMAL SHELTER.

- RESEARCH CRUELTY-FREE COMPANIES THAT DON'T TEST ON ANIMALS.

- FOSTER AN ANIMAL IN NEED.

LEARNING GOALS

Scuba diving? Knitting? Speaking Spanish? Designing websites? Name a few things you've always wanted to learn how to do. Now consider taking these learning goals a step further. If you're interested in learning to scuba dive, maybe you could put those new skills to use by volunteering to help restore coral reefs. If you want to learn to knit, maybe you could knit a scarf for an organization that donates them to homeless veterans in your area. Think about your learning goals and write about how you could use them as a force for good:

_____

_____

_____

_____

_____

_____

_____

_____

_____

_____

_____

_____

_____

THE PERFECTION TRAP

When we think about *changing the world*, it's easy to feel
intimidated. But it's not about being perfect or guilting
ourselves into helping. It's not all-or-nothing. It may feel like we
need to wait until we have extra time or money or a grand plan
to change the world. But the truth is, we all have the tools right
now to begin. We don't need to launch the next big nonprofit
or organize a political movement to do something that really
matters. Think back over what you've written in this journal so
far. Do you notice any patterns or leanings? When you consider
the tools and strengths you have right now, what small steps
do you envision taking to make a difference?

MY VALUES

What values are most important to you? How do you
feel when you live your values and are true to yourself?

MY MANIFESTO

How can you live a life aligned with your values? In the space
below, use the values you identified on the previous page to
brainstorm what you stand for. Then, use the following page
to create a personal manifesto based on what you discover
about yourself.

_____

_____

_____

_____

_____

_____

_____

_____

_____

_____

_____

_____

_____

_____

_____

_____

_____

MY MANIFESTO

I stand for:

I believe in:

I value:

I promise to:

I will work for:

POLITICS—FOR BETTER OR WORSE

Some people consider themselves political junkies and relish the back-and-forth nature of government. Others find politics to be an incessant source of frustration and anger. In what ways do you express your politics? Do you vote? Do you consider voting effective and important? And if you find politics exhausting and confrontational, how can you make your values heard without sacrificing your peace of mind?

_____

_____

_____

_____

_____

_____

_____

_____

_____

_____

_____

_____

_____

_____

_____

_____

JUST BECAUSE
YOU DO NOT TAKE
AN INTEREST
IN POLITICS
DOESN'T MEAN
POLITICS
WON'T TAKE AN
INTEREST IN YOU.

-PERICLES

You can't depend on your eyes when your IMAGINATION is out of focus.

-MARK TWAIN

★ IMAGINATION ★

CREATIVITY, CURIOSITY, INNOVATION

What does *imagination* mean to you, and is it important in your
life? Why? Why is imagination important to the world?

_____

_____

_____

_____

_____

_____

_____

_____

_____

_____

_____

_____

_____

_____

_____

_____

_____

_____

USING MY TIME

It's easy to feel so overwhelmed by the daily tasks of life that we think, *If I don't have time to exercise, walk my dog, eat more salads, and floss my teeth, how on earth will I have time to make a difference in the world?* Time, and how you spend it, is one of the most important aspects of living a balanced life. Consider how you spend your time, and then make the changes necessary to allow more time for your highest priorities. Whether it's calling your representative, writing letters to potential voters, organizing a charitable bake sale, or volunteering at your local food bank, there are many activities that could fit in your allotted time frame.

IF I HAVE AN EXTRA FIFTEEN MINUTES, I CAN:

IF I HAVE AN EXTRA AFTERNOON, I CAN:

IF I HAVE AN EXTRA DAY OR TWO, I CAN:

CONSCIOUS CONSUMPTION

In our day-to-day lives, we are constantly bombarded with advertising urging us to consume, to spend, to buy. On the other hand, we're not regularly encouraged to think of others, to consider how our daily choices affect one another and the world. What would it mean to be conscious of our consumption? In what ways do your spending patterns reflect your values, desires, and hopes for a better world? In what ways can you bring that spending more in line with your true self?

loyalty to petrified opinion
never yet broke a chain or
freed a human soul.
—MARK TWAIN

THAT'S JUST THE WAY THINGS ARE

It's easy to slip into the rut of thinking, *Things will never change because that's just the way they are. That's just the way things have always been.* We go about our daily lives somewhat desensitized to the suffering around us because we don't believe our small efforts will change the big picture. But what if we decided that this petrified way of thinking doesn't serve us any longer? What are three things you want to change—in your own life, in your community, or in the world at large? How can you go about starting to make those changes happen?

_____

_____

_____

_____

_____

_____

_____

_____

_____

_____

_____

_____

_____

FAITH IN HUMANITY

We've all seen movies that make us feel empowered, that show us that the world is beautiful and that even the little guy can take on the giant and win sometimes. Whether it's *Hidden Figures* or *Remember the Titans* or *Erin Brockovich* or *Schindler's List*, which movies renew your faith in humanity? What is it about these stories that inspires you?

_____

_____

_____

_____

_____

_____

_____

_____

_____

_____

_____

_____

_____

_____

_____

_____

❧ HOPE ❧

OPTIMISM, FAITH, CONVICTION

What does *hope* mean to you? Why is it important
in your life? Why is hope important to the world?

_____

_____

_____

_____

_____

_____

_____

_____

_____

_____

_____

_____

_____

_____

_____

_____

_____

_____

_____

_____

_____

MY
RELIGION
IS TO
DO
GOOD.

—THOMAS PAINE

THE RIPPLE EFFECT

One of the benefits of taking action and living our values is that others see this and are inspired to do the same. Both courage and kindness are contagious, and seeing that catch on in others feels pretty good. It helps us to not feel powerless. Which people around you do you see being brave and kind in their lives? Do you see this ripple effect happening around you? How might you inspire others to take action?

_____

_____

_____

_____

_____

_____

_____

_____

_____

_____

_____

_____

_____

_____

MY THANKSGIVING IS PERPETUAL

By regularly recognizing what we are grateful for,
big and small, we can cultivate feelings of hope and
optimism and help prevent burnout. List
what you are thankful for today.

IN MY LIFE:

IN MY TOWN:

IN THE WORLD:

The question is not what you look at, but what you see.

—HENRY DAVID THOREAU

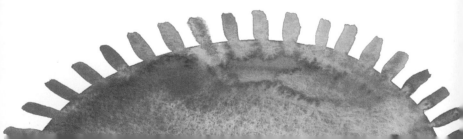

HOPE OVER DESPAIR

Choosing optimism and hope doesn't mean adopting a
Pollyanna approach to life, and ignoring the real and serious
challenges the world faces. Optimism is neither blind nor
naive. It is simply a matter of focus. We can cultivate a feeling
of optimism just by shifting our perspective. When you think
about your general disposition, do you consider yourself an
optimist? A pessimist? A realist? What does this mean to you?
In what ways can you choose hope over despair?

❧ RESPONSIBILITY ❧

RELIABILITY, DEPENDABILITY, INTEGRITY

What does *taking responsibility* mean to you,
and is it important in your life? Why? Why is taking
responsibility important to the world?

_____

_____

_____

_____

_____

_____

_____

_____

_____

_____

_____

_____

_____

_____

_____

_____

WE ARE OUR CHOICES.

-JEAN-PAUL SARTRE

WE ARE OUR CHOICES

Every day we spend money, almost on autopilot. How often
do you really know where your money is going? Pick one
company—grocery chain, utility company, clothing store—
where you regularly spend money, and do a little research.
Does this company share your values? Are their policies
up to your standards?

_____

_____

_____

_____

_____

_____

_____

_____

_____

_____

_____

_____

_____

_____

_____

_____

_____

POSITIVE AFFIRMATIONS

When we feel discouraged, affirmations and encouraging messages really do have a positive effect on our outlook. Do you have a favorite uplifting quote or saying that reminds you to stay positive? Use the space here to write or draw your favorite quote:

The soul
becomes
dyed with
the colors
of its
thoughts.

-MARCUS AURELIUS

QUIET SOLITUDE

Sometimes it feels as if there is endless chatter and noise in our lives. Television, radio, the internet, and social media are constantly throwing ideas, opinions, and sensational headlines our way. We want to be informed citizens, but sometimes all this input negatively affects our mental health. What can we do about it? Making time for quiet solitude can help us sort through the noise and discover what really matters to us.

TAKE A TWO-STEP, PROACTIVE APPROACH:

1. Come up with a plan to limit exposure to news headlines and social media outlets.

2. Develop a stress-reducing practice that helps periodically counteract the noise— meditation, yoga, spending time in nature, breathing exercises, petting an animal. What stress-reducing practices make the most sense to you?

The great use of life is to spend it for something that will outlast it.

-William James

MY MESSAGE

What do you want your life to represent?
What is your message to the world?

_____

_____

_____

_____

_____

_____

_____

_____

_____

_____

_____

_____

_____

_____

_____

_____

_____

_____

_____

We don't have grand, hero to participate in small acts when millions can transform

to engage in

ic actions

the process of change.

multiplied by

# of people,

the world. -HOWARD ZINN

BE A COPYCAT

It's OK to be a copycat. Pay attention to the actions and behavior of others around you. Whether it's being punctual, paying a stranger a compliment, or being extra understanding to a stressed-out cashier, what behaviors do you see in others that you'd like to adopt yourself?

_____

_____

_____

_____

_____

_____

_____

_____

_____

_____

_____

_____

_____

_____

_____

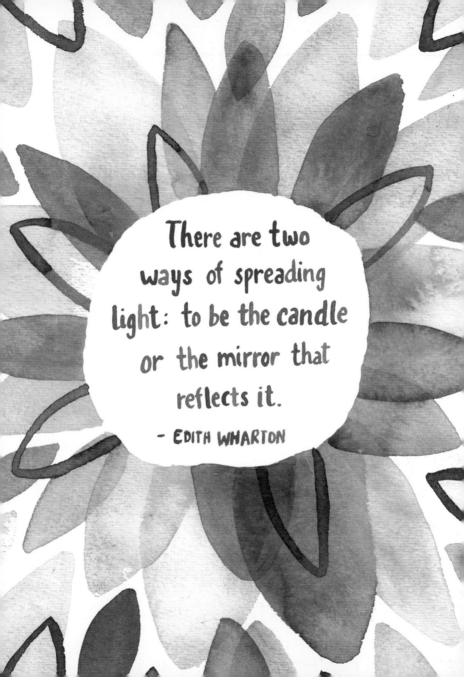

There are two ways of spreading light: to be the candle or the mirror that reflects it.

— EDITH WHARTON

☀ HUMOR ☀

LEVITY, PLAYFULNESS, WHIMSY

What does *humor* mean to you, and is it important in your life?
Why? Why is humor important to the world?

_____

_____

_____

_____

_____

_____

_____

_____

_____

_____

_____

_____

_____

_____

_____

_____

_____

_____

_____

DON'T **SAY** THINGS.
WHAT YOU **ARE** STANDS
OVER YOU THE WHILE,
AND **THUNDERS** SO
THAT I CANNOT HEAR
WHAT YOU SAY
TO THE CONTRARY.

-RALPH WALDO EMERSON

ACTIONS SPEAK LOUDER

Our lives have a voice of their own. Sometimes we convey
messages through our actions that we're not even aware of,
and it can be helpful to have these messages reflected back to
us. Who in your life knows you well enough to help you "hear"
who you are from an outside perspective? Who can you invite,
or trust, to give you an accurate assessment?

_____

_____

_____

_____

_____

_____

_____

_____

_____

_____

_____

_____

_____

_____

_____

_____

_____

_____

IDEAS FOR WAYS TO NARROW YOUR FOCUS.

HOW DO I WANT TO HELP?

ENVIRONMENT:

- **DONATE TO AN ENVIRONMENTAL CHARITY.**

- **RESEARCH WAYS YOU CAN LIMIT YOUR ENVIRONMENTAL IMPACT.**

DWELL IN POSSIBILITY

Nothing creates a feeling of optimism or hope like seeing someone do the impossible. In what ways have you done the impossible in your own life? Have you overcome an obstacle and beaten the odds, even if it's just a small thing, like making it to work on time when you woke up super late? When have you been proud of your perseverance and grit? How can you use that experience to encourage yourself to hold on to that feeling of capability?

_____

_____

_____

_____

_____

_____

_____

_____

_____

_____

_____

_____

_____

_____

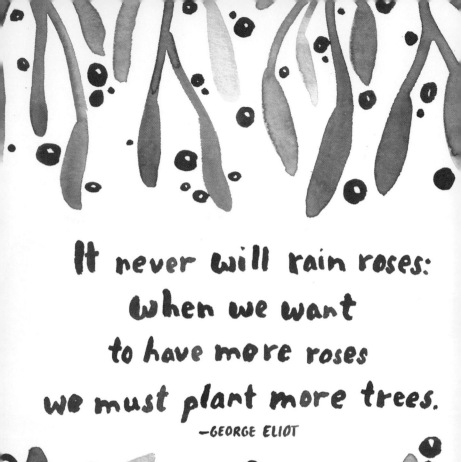

It never will rain roses:
when we want
to have more roses
we must plant more trees.
—GEORGE ELIOT

PLANT MORE ROSES

It's easy to blame big corporations, politicians, or *those people* for the problems we face today. And *those people* hold some of the blame. But if we consider what we can control and examine in our day-to-day choices, we may have more agency than we think. If we're worried about something, what actions are we actually taking to combat it? Are we making our concerns known to our representatives? Are we spreading awareness? Are we making changes in our own lives? What can you do that you're not doing already?

_____

_____

_____

_____

_____

_____

_____

_____

_____

_____

_____

 LEARNING

CURIOSITY, SCHOLARSHIP, WISDOM

What does *learning*—about yourself, about other people,
about how the world works—mean to you, and is it
important in your life? Why? Why is learning important
to the world?

_____

_____

_____

_____

_____

_____

_____

_____

_____

_____

_____

_____

_____

_____

_____

_____

_____

_____

TALENTS ARE BEST
NURTURED IN SOLITUDE :
CHARACTER
IS BEST FORMED
IN THE STORMY
BILLOWS OF THE WORLD.
—JOHANN WOLFGANG
VON GOETHE

BUILDING CHARACTER

How would you describe your character to someone who doesn't know you? What challenges in your life have helped shape your character? In which areas do you want to grow?

_____

_____

_____

_____

_____

_____

_____

_____

_____

_____

_____

_____

_____

_____

_____

_____

_____

_____

_____

_____

VOLUNTEER VACATIONS

Vacations that incorporate learning or working to create a better world can be wonderfully rewarding. They are also a great way to contribute to something important while still enjoying some much-needed time off. For your next vacation, what about helping restore a wildlife habitat, working on an organic farm, volunteering to care for wild animals, or building a school for kids who need one? There are so many opportunities for any kind of trip! Use this space to plan out some locations and activities that you're excited to pursue:

_____

_____

_____

_____

_____

_____

_____

_____

_____

_____

_____

_____

_____

The
unexamined
life is not
worth living.

-Socrates

CREATE AN INSPIRATIONAL MOOD BOARD

Create a tangible, colorful, inspirational bulletin board that
will provide an instant mood boost when you look at it. Include
meaningful quotes, love letters, photos of supportive family
and friends—visual reminders that you are strong, capable, and
ready to take on the world:

CHEERLEADERS

Who are your biggest cheerleaders? Your biggest supporters?
Your mentors? Who will encourage you and guide you as
you work for change?

_____

_____

_____

_____

_____

_____

_____

_____

_____

_____

_____

_____

_____

_____

_____

_____

_____

_____

_____

_____

Be
with
tHose
who
hELp
youR
Being.
—RUMI

CULTIVATE EMPOWERMENT

Just as you can cultivate a feeling of optimism by shifting your focus, you can also cultivate a feeling of empowerment. Taking action, even in small ways, helps boost confidence. Consider what you've written about in this journal so far. What actions do you plan to take on your path to empowerment?

 RESPECT

REVERENCE, ADMIRATION, CIVILITY

What does *respect* mean to you, and is it
important in your life? Why? Why is respect
important to the world?

_____

_____

_____

_____

_____

_____

_____

_____

_____

_____

_____

_____

_____

_____

_____

_____

_____

UNJUST LAWS EXIST: ShALL WE BE CONTENT tO OBEY thEM?

—HENRY DAVID THOREAU

CIVIL DISOBEDIENCE

Some of us are more apt to follow rules, while some of us see rules as mere suggestions. During many periods of struggle in our history, change came about through civil disobedience. How comfortable are you with breaking the rules if you feel it's appropriate? Are there any circumstances where breaking the rules is warranted? Does your passion warrant civil disobedience? What effect do you think this might have?

"HOPE"

IS THE THING WITH
THAT PERCHES IN

—EMILY DICKINSON

FEATHERS -
THE SOUL

MY THANKSGIVING IS PERPETUAL

By regularly recognizing what we are grateful for,
big and small, we can cultivate feelings of hope and
optimism and help prevent burnout. List
what you are thankful for today.

IN MY LIFE:

IN MY TOWN:

IN THE WORLD:

THE GOLDEN RULE

The Golden Rule is universally affirmed within all major religions: Do unto others as you would have them do unto you. It is rooted in the values of human dignity and compassion. And yet, it seems to be one of the more difficult ethical principles to attain. Think about the Golden Rule and what it means to you. How do you apply it in your life? Where do you see it lacking, or being misapplied, either in your own life or elsewhere in the world?

_____

_____

_____

_____

_____

_____

_____

_____

_____

_____

_____

_____

_____

_____

A JOURNEY
OF A THOUSAND
MILES STARTS WITH
A SINGLE STEP.

—LAO TZU

REACH FOR THE STARS

Many famous activists and change makers throughout history—Martin Luther King, Jr., Mahatma Gandhi, Mother Teresa—have become cultural icons. We don't have to be famous to effect change. Ordinary people do amazing things every day. But do you identify with any famous change makers in our history? How do they inspire you?

_____

_____

_____

_____

_____

_____

_____

_____

_____

_____

_____

_____

_____

_____

_____

DANCE AROUND THE LIVING ROOM

Many of us have a favorite song that pumps us up, that helps us power through those last few reps at the gym or summon that last bit of willpower to clean the bathroom. When you need a mood boost and want to dance around the living room, what are your go-to songs to get your blood pumping?

_____

_____

_____

_____

_____

_____

_____

_____

_____

_____

_____

_____

_____

_____

_____

MUSIC IS THE
SHORTHAND
OF EMOTION.
—LEO TOLSTOY

No act of
KINDNESS,
no matter
how SMALL,
is ever
WASTED. ~ Attributed
to Aesop

HEALTH BENEFITS

In case you needed a reason to be a kind soul, studies show that nice people actually live longer, healthier lives! When you think about volunteering for a particular cause, what positive health effects do you hope to gain?

_____

_____

_____

_____

_____

_____

_____

_____

_____

_____

_____

_____

_____

_____

_____

_____

_____

_____

There must
be quite
a few
things a
hot bath
won't cure,
but I don't
know many
of them.

— SYLVIA PLATH

SELF-CARE, OR HOW TO NOT THROW THINGS AT THE TV WHEN YOU WATCH THE NEWS

Over time, the cumulative effect of negative news headlines can be pretty overwhelming and exhausting. It's important that we balance our activism with relaxing ways to nourish ourselves—mind, body, and spirit—for the long haul. Primal scream in an empty car? A hot bath? Double fudge ripple ice cream? When you think of *self-care*, what does that mean to you? What do you do to renew yourself for the struggle?

_____

_____

_____

_____

_____

_____

_____

_____

_____

_____

_____

_____

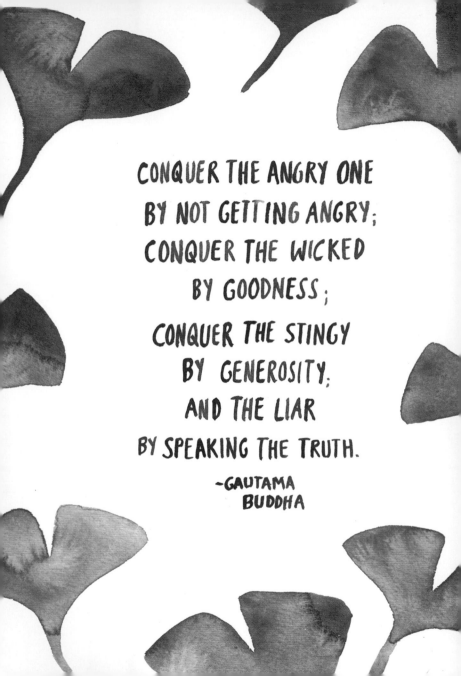

CONQUER THE ANGRY ONE
BY NOT GETTING ANGRY;
CONQUER THE WICKED
BY GOODNESS;
CONQUER THE STINGY
BY GENEROSITY;
AND THE LIAR
BY SPEAKING THE TRUTH.

—GAUTAMA
BUDDHA

RESPOND WITH INTEGRITY

Our interactions with the world may provoke us to respond
in ways that are not conducive to change. Anger may feel like
an appropriate response to actions and beliefs that bump up
against our values, but expressing anger in destructive ways
will not further any cause or help bring people together. How
do you channel your anger in effective ways? How can you
respond with integrity?

_____

_____

_____

_____

_____

_____

_____

_____

_____

_____

_____

_____

_____

_____

_____

_____

_____

REVOLUTIONARY EXPRESSION

Art has long been a site for revolutionary ideas and is especially resonant in times of despair. Whether it's music, poetry, graffiti, or protest signs, what art forms speak to you most powerfully? When you think about your passions and concerns, how might you express them artistically?

IDEAS FOR WAYS TO NARROW YOUR FOCUS.

HOW DO I WANT TO HELP?

PEOPLE (IMMIGRATION, VETERANS AFFAIRS, EDUCATION, DOMESTIC VIOLENCE, PRISON REFORM):

- **DONATE TO AN ORGANIZATION THAT PROVIDES SERVICES TO HOMELESS VETERANS.**

- **VOLUNTEER AT A LOCAL DOMESTIC VIOLENCE SHELTER.**

This is no time
for ease and
comfort.

It's time to
dare and endure.
-WINSTON CHURCHILL

DARE AND ENDURE

Deciding to advocate for change takes courage, and sometimes it can invite criticism and even backlash. When you consider the most pressing issues in the world today, who are the role models who are taking the lead and finding solutions? Have they overcome hardship? Are they enduring criticism for taking a stand? What can you learn from them? How do they inspire you to continue on your own path?

 JUSTICE

FAIRNESS, LAWFULNESS, EQUITY

What does *justice* mean to you, and is
it important in your life? Why? Why is justice
important to the world?

_____

_____

_____

_____

_____

_____

_____

_____

_____

_____

_____

_____

_____

_____

_____

_____

_____

_____

The arc of the **moral** universe is long, but it bends toward justice.

-MARTIN LUTHER KING, JR.

SELF-COMPASSION

We can't take care of others unless we take care of ourselves
first. You need a strong foundation in order to be in it for the
long haul and avoid burnout. Self-compassion is a good place
to begin. What does self-compassion look like to you?

I AM LARGER,
BIGGER THAN I
THOUGHT; I DID NOT
KNOW I HELD SO
MUCH GOODNESS.

-WALT WHITMAN

STAYCATION

Schedule some alone time, whatever your budget and
schedule allow—an afternoon, a long weekend, or a whole
week dedicated to slowing down with discernment. With no
appointments or obligations, how do you find yourself
spending your time? What do you lean toward?

_____

_____

_____

_____

_____

_____

_____

_____

_____

_____

_____

_____

_____

_____

_____

_____

_____

where there is
CHARITY
and
WISDOM,
there is neither
FEAR
nor
IGNORANCE.
— SAINT FRANCIS OF
ASSISI

THE BIGGER PICTURE

When we act for the sake of other people, or for the bigger
picture, we know in our hearts that we stand on the right side
of history. Sometimes the antidote to our fear is understanding
it. Take an issue that makes you anxious or fearful and really
explore it. Consider all angles and perspectives. What do you
notice when you step back and consider the bigger picture?

_____

_____

_____

_____

_____

_____

_____

_____

_____

_____

_____

_____

_____

_____

_____

_____

IT'S A FAMILY AFFAIR

Take one issue you care about and unite your family—biological or chosen—around it. Maybe it's encouraging others to unite around a common cause, or maybe it's joining a group of people who are already fired up about the same cause as you. Do you have a cause that comes to mind? Do you have a group of folks you could rally? How might you combine the two?

BE A ROLE MODEL

Children learn a lot from observing the adults in their lives. They gain confidence and character by doing things that matter and are inspired by watching you take risks. What kind of role model do you want to be? What values are important for you to share?

_____

_____

_____

_____

_____

_____

_____

_____

_____

_____

_____

_____

_____

_____

_____

_____

_____

_____

It is
in the sh
each oth
the People

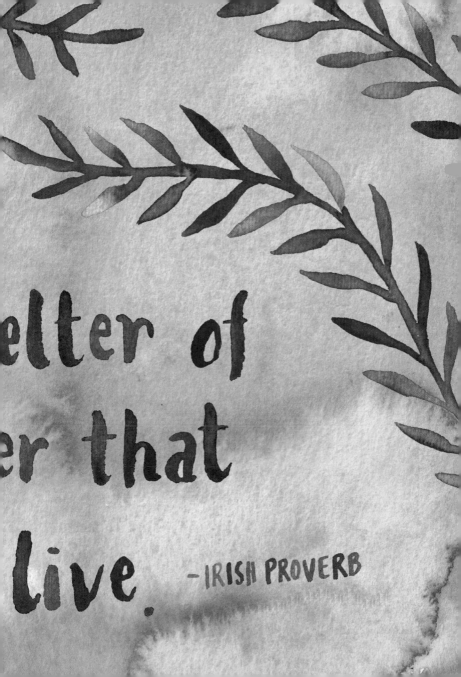

elter of
er that
live. –IRISH PROVERB

Whoever gives reverence receives reverence.

—RUMI

WISDOM IS THE REWARD

By the time we're adults, we're pretty clear on how we feel
about the most pressing issues in the world. We're certain
in our beliefs, have our argument prepared, and know who's
to blame. But the importance of being right often keeps us
from understanding one another. Taking the time to listen and
really understand someone else's viewpoint is an exercise in
patience and respect. Sometime soon, have a conversation
with someone you disagree with. Be mindful of your desire to
convince this person of your point of view, and really try to
hear where they are coming from. How does this make you
feel? Do you notice any common ground? Write down what
you learned and the impact it had on your beliefs:

FOR INTROVERTS

If you're an introvert, participating in a protest march or calling your representative might not feel comfortable. But there are many different ways to engage. Sign a petition. Write an op-ed for a newspaper explaining your opposition to or support for a cause. Create a piece of art—a song, a play, a sermon—and share it. Use this space to brainstorm your ideas:

EVERYONE THINKS
OF CHANGING
the world, but
NO ONE THINKS
OF CHANGING
himself. —LEO
TOLSTOY

CHANGE WITHIN

When you think of the changes that need to be made in the
world, do you also identify changes that need to be made within
you? How do you think those changes will affect your sense of
well-being? How will they affect the people around you?

 PERSEVERANCE

PERSISTENCE, TENACITY, RESOLUTION

What does *perseverance* mean to you, and is it
important in your life? Why? Why is perseverance
important to the world?

_____

_____

_____

_____

_____

_____

_____

_____

_____

_____

_____

_____

_____

_____

_____

_____

_____

_____

IN THEIR HONOR

Think of a family member or friend who is no longer living. Did they have a cause they were passionate about? Could you make a donation or volunteer in their honor?

_____

_____

_____

_____

_____

_____

_____

_____

_____

_____

_____

_____

_____

_____

_____

_____

_____

_____

MY THANKSGIVING IS PERPETUAL

By regularly recognizing what we are grateful for,
big and small, we can cultivate feelings of hope and
optimism and help prevent burnout. List
what you are thankful for today.

IN MY LIFE:

IN MY TOWN:

IN THE WORLD:

AS TO ME
I KNOW OF
NOTHING
ELSE BUT
MIRACLES.

-WALT
WHITMAN

A BETTER FUTURE

Faith, trust, the belief that change *can* happen . . .
What fuels your hope for a better future?

_____

_____

_____

_____

_____

_____

_____

_____

_____

_____

_____

_____

_____

_____

_____

_____

_____

_____

_____

_____

_____

_____